BRIAR MOUTH

Helen Nicholson

HAPPENSTANCE

Poems © Helen Nicholson, 2018
Cover image © Gillian Rose, 2018
ISBN 978-1-910131-46-6
All rights reserved

ACKNOWLEDGMENTS:

Thanks to the editors of the following magazines, in which some of these poems, or versions of poems, appeared: *Gutter*, *Magma*. 'Summer House' was short-listed in the Bridport International Creative Writing Competition, 2015.

'Light Fantastic' was commissioned by Professor Robert Crawford, University of St Andrews, as part of a project for the UNESCO International Year of Light, 2015.

'Elegy' is a found poem, with text selected from entries in *The Illustrated Gaelic-English Dictionary* by Edward Dwelly. The poem is in memory of my father, a Gaelic speaker from the Isle of Skye.

Many thanks to all fellow poets and tutors for valued and constructive criticism over the years, most recently: members of Ceres Poets, University of St Andrews MLitt/MFA workshops and Mimi Khalvati's Poetry School workshops.

Printed by The Dolphin Press
www.dolphinpress.co.uk

First published in 2018 by Happen*Stance* Press,
21 Hatton Green, Glenrothes, Fife KY7 4SD
nell@happenstancepress.com
www.happenstancepress.com

CONTENTS

This Room / 5
Briar Mouth / 6
Speech Therapy / 7
Additions to a Glaze / 8
Elegy / 9
My Bonnie Prince / 10
Haars and Sea Frets / 11
A Family History / 12
Scarves / 16
Softening / 17
Lodestone / 18
The Sound of It / 19
Big Man / 20
Heroic Couplets with Handkerchief / 21
Light Fantastic / 22
Sticks and Stones / 23
Woodcarver / 24
Gaelic Learners' Exam / 25
Second Home / 26
Advice to Students of 'Gaelic Cultural Studies' / 27
The Poem's Complaint / 28

For all my teachers

THIS ROOM

So after all that, after all,
that is my job. I know it now.
I'd thought it in the next room
but one. Always a door ajar,
a calling breeze. But now I know
it's here—as shiny, lush and green
as that ground elder anointed with rain.
Some leaves have a mirror sheen.
Others stare, mottled, but not the dull
I'd made them. So, that's my job:
this small room, this window view.
This shiver of cold.

BRIAR MOUTH

Had I been   granted   pebbles in my m   outh
I would have   dis   bursed my   g   ift long ago
But I was   granted   brambles

Thorns n   icked but it   wasn't all
b   loody   Occasional soft dark   fruit
p   ushed   past the alveolar   ridge

I would un   tie my   tongue   (I could
sometimes)   tease each   bramble
round my hard   palate   then my soft

until a   burst   drupelet would tr   ickle
its   juice   back down   my   throat
Little es   c   aped my   lips

I allowed a   few en   chanted
fav   ourite   sounds to   roll   mutely
back and   forth   back and   forth

Carse of Gowrie
Carse of Gowrie
Carse of Gowrie

Helen Nicholson

SPEECH THERAPY

It's hard to confuse a pimp with pumpernickel
though some might try. The pith in the teeth
and the urge to spit make it seem easy.

But it's not. Mark my words and my presence
in heaven. Pray I won't get there before I can
sweeten most meat with cinnamon and kale.

Kale sweetens? But not when you want it to.
Most times the 'k' sticks in my throat, won't
slide past my lips without a kick under the table.

The 'c' in cinnamon won't escape easy either.
That simple adder swells to anaconda,
s   s   s   lowly.

Say it sing-song: ride the dragon, breathe fire,
pretend you're from Alabama or Abalone,
offer up gurgles, growls, gutturals, fricatives.

Sugar beet turns belly-fat sour if sizzled at dawn.
Star anise gives a green edge to that exquisite
hardness of tooth by the gum. Mark my words.

ADDITIONS TO A GLAZE

I was good at slicing lemon pith.
I'd take a sharp knife, thin blade,
and shave that spongy layer
until all white was pared away.

Lemon oil oozed against the steel,
as was the case with orange oil,
though that threatened exuberance,
the possibility of sweetness.

Wasn't the trick not to waste
anything? Goosebumps appeared
closer to the outer skin; it was my
job, my mission, to render them null.

Then my knife was ready for slicing
into precise matchsticks the orange
and yellow accoutrements. For that
is all they were.

ELEGY

i.m. Kenny John Nicholson, 12.08.1911 - 17.02.1968

feadag, feadaige, feadagan (n, f)
    a plover
    a flute, a whistle
    the third week in February

eile, eile (n, f)
    an oration
    a prayer, an entreaty
    the lowing of deer

an sàs (adv)
    hooked
    in custody
    embedded, as a needle in cloth

sùgh, sùgha, sùghan (n, m)
    juice, sap, moisture
    sense, meaning
    dearest object, darling
    huge receding wave

MY BONNIE PRINCE

I most loved the cool, undulating blue
of your coat, your kilt and your buckles
(a relic from my Bobby Shaftoe phase).

In my dreams your bonnet was soft as felt,
a deeper blue; you held it at your side.
I knew you had come for me, cap in hand

despite your kingly claims. How proud I was
to take you back to Glenfinnan, show you
your monument and viaduct after the Games.

Back home, star of the Cocktail Bar display,
your mirrored back crossed belt and sash.
Oh Charlie, you cut a dash and you knew it.

Then I let you share my bath. Not even goodbye
before you made off. They say you're now in Skye.

---

1   Plaster statuettes of Bonnie Prince Charlie, distributed by Drambuie, were intended for display in licensed premises, not for immersion in hot water.

Helen Nicholson

HAARS AND SEA FRETS

A haar is cold.
A sea fret may not be.
It may hold warmth.
Or it may not.
But a haar
will never warm you.

A FAMILY HISTORY

i

Andrew Hamilton According to his Proverbs

Never seek a wife till ye ken what to do wi' her.
Nathing to be done in haste but gripping of fleas.

ii

Helen Hamilton in Old Age, 1961

Here is the image of your damp old age:
a whispery blue chiffon scarf, polka dots
machine-stamped in stiff, pure white,
taupe wool-rib stockings, rolled tight
to the knee. Frayed elastic and thick slippers.
You peed majestically onto the fire rug—
great streams of hallowed piss. I can still hear
the torrent, inhale the lift of a baggy skirt.

Tucked into your corner cot you told me
your visions of the Baby Jesus, calling you,
Helen Hamilton from Hamilton, possessed
of the best-turned ankles in Hamilton,
wife to the carter's son from Riccarton,
now in Hell. Him. His name never spoken.

iii

Naming Protocol

John, the cabinet maker,
rubs linseed gently
on a secret drawer,
for the memory
of his older John.
Helen, the milliner,
tiptoes round the shades
of Ellen and Helen.
And all the while,
their mother muffles them
with handkerchiefs
and their burden of names.

iv

On My Father's Side

My great grandfather's brothers
carried his kist barefoot,
the water's chill on their toes,
a wreath of toe-tacks on his coffin lid
as they bore him inchmeal,
safe, to the other side.

SCARVES

For going out, a nice scarf does the trick.
You know the sort of thing, often a gift:
a good weave, abstract, not too flashy—
a scarf that fits in, cheers a neutral suit,
brings out what's left of warm skin tones.

For staying in, I lock the door. The key
to the drawer is tucked under the stairtread.
I tiptoe, catch my breath. Click. Slide my hand
among chiffon, chenille, crêpe de Chine.
My best scarves are not for your eyes.

A fabulous silk unfolds its smooth
narrative, one slight abrasive
slub the twist in its tale. A murmured
conversation with bruised velvet teaches me
the curve of my collar bone. Texture is text.

A feather boa rims the graduation robes
I have spun from air. I strut a little
but—tamed by cashmere—turn my back
on vanity. I do not need empty eyes
feeding on me. It is dark. I learn by feel.

I trail on my hand, my neck, my lip, my lobe
the quiet insistent braille of devoré.

SOFTENING

The day you died, we'd a soft
argument about guillemot wings.
You won. I like to think I let you.

I never saw a guillemot, nor
its wings. Nor was there a 'you'
or a 'we' in such proximity.

But, my dear, it is such a comfort
to imagine us, our shy wings
untied—us, unstoppable,
bickering about lanolin.

LODESTONE

lonestone
greystone hardstone
eggstone speckledstone
smoothstone curvingstone
curlingstone pivotstone perfectstone
polishedstone surfacestone
shellstone shorestone
oldstone coldstone
unknownstone

THE SOUND OF IT

Say 'three blind mice'
and you're on an upbeat.
It's not just the gleeful echo
or the plinky-plink school piano.
You know, when you repeat yourself,
these guys are going somewhere.

Say 'three dead fledglings'
and the organ stop is muffled.
You're already turning your face away,
dropping tissues as shrouds on the grass,
feeling with a poo-bag pulled over your hand
the first body for the bin, thrapple to tail,
with a prayer for the unsung song.

BIG MAN

He was a big man,
Pat Quinn, big-bellied but strong.
He roared for his pint

and shouted the odds
alone, by the Guinness tap.
Overspilled his verse

and his emotions:
a stamping bull if slighted,
babied with soft words.

Caruso at closing time,
bone dry for Lent. Off the site,
proud of his spick flat.

And his span? Too short.
He clutched at his sheet, shrunken,
knuckle-scared by death.

HEROIC COUPLETS WITH HANDKERCHIEF

To write the perfect parody of Pope
You need more graft and steely wit than hope.
If cribbing from *The Dunciad* won't pass
Don't dream of scribbling on the bus, pre-class.
It won't suffice to find a ready rhyme—
Such stratagem's sub-standard, not sublime.

To match the jewel of the Enlightenment
Employ 'strong sense' and rigorous argument.
Don't look to Latin or to Strawberry Hill
For inspiration. Look round. Take your fill
Of sleazy deals, small hurts, and all that's vile
On which it's fruitful to expend your bile.

And if you think your foggy, snot-filled brain
Is master to the task, then think again.

LIGHT FANTASTIC

For Francisco Tenopalo Carmona and the University of St Andrews Laboratory for Biophysics and Biomolecular Dynamics and Organic Semiconductor Optoelectronics Group

So that we may casually flick the light switch,
you must guide your electrons' optimal excitement.

Allow me to be their dancing master. My band
is four-square reliable. You can re-run the results.

High above the Forth I am birling on girders
I choose my own beat, risky as I please.

I can teach them rumba, conga, zopetto, fandango,
bolero, Concheros, El Jarabe Tapatío.

Or take your partners for an Orcadian 'Strip the Willow'.
Born of the Northern Lights, the mirrie dancers pull together.

Dazzled polymers birl in a chain perpetual. Their tiny
hands clap as they gain their second wind.

STICKS AND STONES

At school they call him 'The Sgadan'.
He helps his mother gut the fish.
Her blade slits each silver belly,
his forefinger scoops the guts.
He sits alone in the last row,
the silent stink at the back.

'Jellicoe' sits proud in the front row.
His mother minds the village shop.
She pats salt butter under water,
keeps a stub of lipstick on the counter
and a compact of pressed powder
for when her sailor will return.

Sgadan—herring

WOODCARVER

i.m. Grinling Gibbons (1648-1721)

I shall run my finger along the grain, hear
the knock on the heart, choose when to fret
or gouge. I shall know when a fishtail or skew
is called for and the why of a ferrule or tang.
It will take time. I am willing to breathe long,
contort and bend, an apprentice to my wood.

I shall learn the scent of limewood, of linden,
and the function of finger, palm and eye in grip.
When even my shavings curl smooth, I'll make
my world an oyster, rosecurl, peapod, feather
in pliant wood. I shall design, for ten years hence,
a reredos before which I'll lay this chiselled plate.

When I become my Master's master, I shall feel
my bosting knife and my double bevel blade
firm in my hand. My wrens will sing, grapes blush,
anemones bow their heads, then tilt toward the sun.
When you grasp the brittle twist of my laurel leaf,
you'll resist its crisp decay, and think on yours.

GAELIC LEARNERS' EXAM

1

On the island
The stilted stagger of hind legs,
a black tadpole-wriggling tail.
A lamb sucks a head-butted udder.
The still-warm skin of the stillborn
is his cover.

2

It is a question of fit:
the placing of an accent;
the placing of myself
—mi fhìn—in the sentence.
I suck a Polo mint,
tongue the brittle edge.

SECOND HOME

I never met who owned the summer house
I helped to clean those years ago on Skye.
My cousin held the key. I didn't pry
but open shelves invited me to browse.

Whose mind, I asked, was calmed or was aroused
by Kant, Disraeli, Montesquieu and Bly?
I puzzled at his contradictions—why
he owned a gun, but page-marked 'To a Mouse'.

Binoculars for otter, seals or deer
lay slung beside his monkish truckle bed
by photos of the house in Belgrave Square.
It's only now the need for both seems clear.

Whole days expended in my garden shed
show part of me lives here, and part lives there.

ADVICE TO STUDENTS OF
'GAELIC CULTURAL STUDIES'

Next time you knock on the door
of an old lady with good Gaelic,
renowned as a tradition-bearer,
who, four miles from the main road,
looks out to Canna, Eigg and Rum—
once you've established your connections
and that, no, she never used a *cas-chrom*
and, no, she can't say she, personally,
saw the *each-uisge* at Lochan Dubh;
once you've praised her hot buttered scones,
and slipped in *co-dhiùs* as common ground;
then, when you feel warm enough to ask
what she misses most from the old days—
don't show surprise if it is trying on hats
in Arnott's, Pettigrew's and Copland & Lye.

cas-chrom—foot plough
each-uisge—mythical water horse, kelpie; malign shape-shifter (sometimes appearing as a handsome man)
co-dhiù—however, whether, whatever

THE POEM'S COMPLAINT

My dear! Can you imagine the stink?
All those, all those *fish*—their rotting spindle bones
sticking out between my stanzas. And those fins!
Don't talk to me about fins—spineless webby fans.
Honestly! I retch at the thought of fluttering gills.
Then there's the *obh, obh* Celtic twilight-y nonsense,
hankering after sunsets and crags, and crooning.
Always the Cuillin—that's *Coo-lin*. And more fish.
Herring mostly. *Clupea harengus*. Where's the fun
in this? She used to, you know. Joke. Now all po-
faced and rhyming. No—not the dreaded couplets—
at least old wooden nose pegs keep out the stink.

obh, obh—exclamation: oh dear! good heavens!